A Bean's Life

Angela Royston

Published 2011 by
A&C Black Publishers Ltd.
36 Soho Square, London, W1D 3QY

www.acblack.com

ISBN   HB 978-1-4081-3391-0
         PB 978-1-4081-3390-3

Text copyright © 2010 Angela Royston

This book is produced using paper that is made from wood grown in managed, sustainable forests. It is natural, renewable and recyclable. The logging and manufacturing processes conform to the environmental regulations of the country of origin.

Produced for A&C Black by Calcium. www.calciumcreative.co.uk

Printed and bound in China by C&C Offset Printing Co.

All the internet addresses given in this book were correct at the time of going to press. The author and publishers regret any inconvenience caused if addresses have changed or sites have ceased to exist, but can accept no responsibility for any such changes.

Acknowledgements

The publishers would like to thank the following for their kind permission to reproduce their photographs:

Cover: Shutterstock
Pages: Dreamstime: Darko Plohl 14–15; Photolibrary: Jeronimo Alba 18, Rex Butcher 16, Howard Rice 12; Shutterstock: Arteretum 11, Artography 4, Bonchan 20, Nito 1, 15, Optimarc 19, Orientaly 6, Orla 9, Piotrwrk 13, SeDmi 15, Sevenke 3, 5, Alex Staroseltsev 17, Superdumb 21, Bogdan Wankowicz 7, 8, 10.

Contents

What are Beans?

Beans come from plants. Many different types of bean are grown around the world – this book is about broad beans.

Why are beans grown?

People grow beans because they are good to eat and can taste delicious when they are cooked. They also contain **vitamins** that keep your body healthy.

Baked beans

Baked beans are made from a type of bean called the haricot bean.

Broad beans have a thick, green skin.

Colours and shapes

Different types of bean look different. Many beans are red, some are round, while other beans look like tiny eggs.

Planting Beans

Beans are **seeds** as well as food, so when a bean is planted in the soil, it grows into a plant. The plant then makes more beans.

Where do beans grow?

Broad beans grow well in cool countries. They are planted at the end of winter and can stand very cold weather. Beans are planted in long rows in the soil.

Tough stuff

Broad bean plants can grow even when the soil is covered with snow.

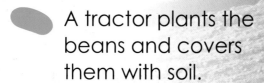

A tractor plants the beans and covers them with soil.

Below the soil

Inside the bean is a tiny plant. As the bean lies in the soil, the tiny plant begins to grow.

Growing in the Soil

The bean is a **store** of food that the tiny plant uses to grow bigger and bigger. After a while, the tiny plant is too big to stay inside the bean, and it bursts out of the bean's skin.

What happens next?

A **root** pushes through the skin and grows down into the soil. A green **shoot** pokes through the top of the bean and grows upwards through the soil.

Shoot

To the sun

Broad bean shoots grow upwards towards the sunlight at the soil's surface.

Roots and a shoot grow into the soil.

Root

Thirsty plants

A plant needs water to grow. Its roots are covered with thin hairs that take in water from the soil.

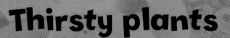

Root

Breaking Through

After a few weeks, the shoot is so long that it pushes through the top of the soil. Two small leaves open up at the end of the **stem**.

Why do leaves grow?

As the stem grows taller, more leaves grow. The plant has finished the food stored in the bean, so the leaves make food for the plant instead.

Stem

Skin

Empty skin

The empty bean skin falls into the soil and **rots** away.

The bean plant breaks through the surface of the soil.

Tube

Making food

Leaves make sugary juice from water, sunlight, and air. The juice travels along tiny tubes to the rest of the plant.

Flowers

The plant grows taller and taller and, after a few weeks, **buds** grow on the stem. They open up into small flowers.

Bees like flowers!

Bees crawl into the flowers. Inside each flower is yellow **pollen** dust, which sticks to the bees' legs and is then carried to other flowers.

Lots of flowers grow close together on the stems.

Bud

Hairy bees

Bees have very hairy legs! Pollen sticks to the hairs when bees land on flowers.

Pollen

Honey bee

Flowers contain a sweet juice called **nectar**. Bees make honey from nectar to store inside their nests.

Green Pods

After the flowers have died and the petals have fallen off, a thin green **pod** grows beneath the dying flower. The pod contains tiny beans.

Why did the beans grow?

Each tiny bean grew after it joined with a grain of pollen from another flower. The beans grow bigger and the pods grow longer.

The pods grow where the flowers used to be.

How many beans?

Most broad bean pods contain between three and eight broad beans.

Safe inside

The pod is tough on the outside and fluffy on the inside to protect the growing beans.

Pod

Attack!

Bean beetles and other **insects** eat the leaves of the plant. Hundreds of beetles can feed on just one plant.

Blackflies harm beans

Blackflies also feed on bean plants. They suck juice called **sap** from inside the plant.

Fight back

Some farmers use **chemicals** to kill the insects that attack their broad bean plants.

Blackflies crowd together under a leaf.

Farmers' friends

Farmers like ladybirds because they love to eat the blackflies.

Blackfly

Time to Pick

It is three or four months since the seeds were planted, and the pods are now long and fat. They are ready to be picked.

How are the beans picked?
Farmers use special machines to pick the pods. The machine pulls up the plants from the soil and shakes the beans off the plants.

The machines pick the beans in rows.

Into the soil
The plants are dug back into the soil once the beans have been picked.

Eat some, keep some

The beans are picked when they are sweet and juicy. Some beans are kept as seeds for next year.

To the Shops

Most broad beans are sold as food for people to eat. They are taken to a factory, where they are washed and cooked.

How are beans stored?

Some of the beans are put into cans. The rest are frozen and put in plastic bags. The cans and bags are taken in trucks to shops and supermarkets.

You can buy beans that are still fresh in their pods.

Open up

You have to split open the pod to reach the beans.

Buying beans

You can buy frozen beans, canned beans, or beans in jars.

Fresh beans

Glossary

buds flowers before they open

chemicals substances that affect things. Chemicals can be used to kill pests such as insects.

insects small animals with six legs

nectar sweet juice made by flowers

pod container that holds seeds while they form

pollen yellow dust found in the centre of flowers

root part of a plant that takes in water

rots begins to break up

sap watery fluid that is found inside plants' stems

seeds part of the fruit of a plant. A seed can grow into a new plant.

shoot the first two leaves and stem of a plant

stem part of a plant from which leaves, flowers and fruit grow

store to keep something, or a place where something is kept

vitamins tiny parts of food that keep the body healthy

Further Reading

Websites

Find out how to grow your own bean plant at:
www.greatgrubclub.com/grow-a-bean-plant

Click on the pictures to see how a plant grows at:
www.zephyrus.co.uk/seed.html

Books

Life Cycles: Beans by Melanie Mitchell,
Lerner (2003).

Life Cycles: Broad Bean by Louise Spilsbury,
Raintree (2003).

The Life Cycle of a Bean by Linda Tagliaferro,
Pebble Plus (2007).

The Life Cycle of a Bean by Ruth Thomson,
Wayland (2007).

Index